W9-DJG-330

THE SPACE EXPLORER'S GUIDE TO

Earth's Neighborhood

SPACE UNIVERSITY™

BY **HENA KHAN**

WITH **RACHEL CONNOLLY**
SPACE EDUCATOR

RYAN WYATT
VISUAL ADVISOR

AND **JIM SWEITZER**, Ph.D.
NASA SCIENCE CENTER,
DePaul UNIVERSITY

SCHOLASTIC INC.

NEW YORK   TORONTO   LONDON   AUCKLAND   SYDNEY
MEXICO CITY   NEW DELHI   HONG KONG   BUENOS AIRES

Who's Who at Space U

Hena Khan
Writer

Hena is a writer who lives in a little corner of Earth's neighborhood known as Maryland with her husband and son.

Rachel Connolly
Consultant

Rachel manages the astrophysics education program at the American Museum of Natural History's Rose Center for Earth and Space.

Ryan Wyatt
Visual Advisor

Ryan designs scientific visuals for the American Museum of Natural History's Rose Center for Earth and Space.

Jim Sweitzer
Advisor

Jim is an astrophysicist and the director of the NASA Space Science Center at DePaul University in Chicago.

ISBN: 0-439-55741-0

Copyright © 2003 by Scholastic Inc.

Editor: Andrea Menotti
Assistant Editor: Megan Gendell
Designers: Peggy Gardner, Lee Kaplan, Roberta Melzl, Robert Rath, Tracey Schmitt
Illustrators: Daniel Aycock, Yancey C. Labat, Thomas Nackid, Ed Shems

Photos:
Front cover: The Earth rising over the Moon, as seen by the *Apollo 8* astronauts (image by NASA).
Back cover: An image of the extreme ultraviolet light produced by the Sun, taken by the SOHO spacecraft (Solar and Heliospheric Observatory). You can learn more about ultraviolet light, which is invisible to the human eye, on page 14 (image by SOHO/ESA/NASA).
Title page: An *Apollo 17* astronaut next to a large boulder on the Moon.
All interior images are by NASA unless otherwise noted below.
Pages 5, 7, 8, 9, 10, 11, 13, and 23: Images by SOHO (ESA & NASA). Page 9 (close-up view of sunspots): G. Sharmer (ISP, RSAS, Lockheed-Martin Solar and Astrophysics Lab). Pages 4–5, 18, and 40 (Earth): R. Stockli/Robert Simmon/NASA GFC/MODIS. Pages 4, 27, 28, 32, and 47 (full Moon): NASA/JPL/USGS. Page 17: Sheila Terry/Photo Researchers. Page 24: (top) J. Finch/Photo Researchers. (background image) Pekka Parviainen/Photo Researchers. Page 29: David Nunuk/Photo Researchers. Page 38 (meteorite): Detlev Ravenswaay/Photo Researchers. Page 38 (Meteor Crater): David Parker/Photo Researchers. Page 44: NASA Johnson Space Center, Orbital Debris Program Office.

All rights reserved. Published by Scholastic Inc. No part of this publication may be reproduced, stored in a retrieval system, or transmitted in any form or by any means, electronic, mechanical, photocopying, recording, or otherwise, without the prior written permission of the publisher. For information regarding permission, write to Scholastic Inc., Attention: Permissions Department, 557 Broadway, New York, NY 10012.

SCHOLASTIC, SPACE UNIVERSITY, and associated logos are trademarks and/or registered trademarks of Scholastic Inc.

12 11 10 9 8 7 6 5 4 3 2 1   3 4 5 6 7 8/0

Printed in the U.S.A.

First Scholastic printing, November 2003

The publisher has made every effort to ensure that the activities in this book are safe when done as instructed. Adults should provide guidance and supervision whenever the activity requires.

Table of **Contents**

Home Sweet Home

There's no place like home, is there, cadet? Well, you have a much bigger home than you ever imagined—in space, that is! Even though space is huge, empty, and endless, you've got your own little corner of it to call your own. In it you've got your comfy home planet, your energy-giving Sun, and your nighttime pal, the Moon. But even though you've been living in this space neighborhood for your whole life, how well do you really know it? Did you know that:

- You live at the bottom of an ocean over 90 miles (145 km) deep? (An ocean of air, that is, that flows and waves just like water!)

- The Sun has violent storms that can cause blackouts here on Earth?

- We only see one side of the Moon from Earth, and it wasn't until 1959 that we got our first pictures of the far side?

- A few billion years ago, an entire day on Earth was only six hours long? (Because the Earth used to spin faster than it does now!)

- There are over 100,000 pieces of garbage (like screws, bolts, paint chips, and other junk) orbiting Earth, left over from space missions?

- The Moon is slowly spiraling away from us about an inch every year?

- The Moon used to look a lot bigger in the sky, when it was closer?

...in Space!

And that's not all—we've got a lot more juice on your space neighbors! This month, Space U will give you a brand new look at the things you've known your whole life—things like days and nights, Moon phases, and seasons. You'll gain a new understanding of how everything is moving and shaking, spinning and whirling through the universe. You'll also visit places you've never been—like the center of the Earth and the far side of the Moon!

Plus you'll get the answers to a bunch of questions like these:

 What makes the sky blue?

 What do satellites see when they look down on Earth?

 How do we know what's inside the center of the Earth without digging into it?

 What is "syzygy"?

 What happens when an astronaut loses a tool during a space walk?

 What are the weirdest things humans have left behind on the Moon?

Are you ready? With loads of cool facts stored away in your noggin, you'll soon be set for the rest of your space adventures—whether you stick around the neighborhood or venture out to other planets, or beyond!

This month you've been issued some great gear for your neighborhood tour. You've got:

- **A gyroscope.** Just wait till this spinning sensation gets going—it'll balance on your finger, and it'll fight back if you try to turn it upside down! Gyroscopes are important parts of satellites— whirl over to page 41 to find out why!

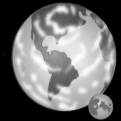

- **An inflatable Earth.** Great news—now you can blow up your home planet! (Just kidding!) Seriously, blow up the Earth and head over to pages 22, 28, or 34 to have some fun with it.

- **A model Moon.** This Moon is exactly the right size to go with your inflatable Earth. Turn to page 35 to get your Moon into orbit!

- **A pack of UV detector beads.** These little guys will change color when they detect invisible UV light from the Sun! Catch some serious rays on page 14!

THE SPACE UNIVERSITY WEB SITE

Don't forget to drop by the Space U web site (www.scholastic.com/space), where you can get to know Earth's neighbors even better. You can see raging solar storms, take part in the Moon Olympics (and hopefully bring home the gold!), and check out today's space weather! Just remember to bring along this month's password, which you can find right here on Planet Password.

PLANET PASSWORD

This month's web site password is:

SUNNYMOON

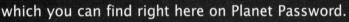

Complete this month's web challenges to earn your personalized mission patch, which you can paste right here.

A Great Ball of Fire!

IT'S A SUPERSTAR!

It's hard to imagine that the Sun is a star, just like the ones you see twinkling in the night sky—but it is! The difference is that the stars you see at night are trillions of miles away from Earth, while the Sun is millions of times closer.

Compared to other stars, our Sun is actually just an average-sized star. But that doesn't make it less than a superstar in *our* world! The Sun is the biggest thing in our solar system—bigger than all the planets and moons combined. In fact, you could pour 1,300,000 (that's 1.3 *million*) Earths into the Sun!

This is an image of the Sun in ultraviolet light that has been colored orange. See page 13 for more on this! And to see how the Sun looks in *visible* light, turn to page 9!

FEELING HOT! HOT! HOT!

The Sun is made of gases, mainly hydrogen and helium. This big ball of gas actually spins around, like the Earth. The whole Sun doesn't spin at the same speed though—it spins fastest around its middle. It takes about 24 days for the middle of the Sun to spin around once, and about 32 days for the poles.

Although we can't see inside the Sun, we know it works like this: Lots and lots of atoms smash into each other and join together in the center of the Sun, creating a huge amount of energy. This energy gets knocked around inside the Sun for tens of millions of years before it reaches the surface and breaks free. Then it takes eight minutes to speed through space before you see it or feel it on your skin!

Sun Smarts!

Never ever look directly at the Sun! It could severely damage your eyes!

In this picture, the Sun is hidden by a black disk. That's because the camera needs to block out the super-bright Sun in order to be able to see the full corona.

Corona

IT'S LIKE A HEATWAVE

The Sun has an atmosphere that extends for several million miles out into space. The outer part of the atmosphere is known as the corona—the glow around the Sun. The corona is extremely hot, even hotter than the surface of the Sun. It has cooler spots, known as coronal holes, where solar wind escapes from the Sun. Wondering what a solar breeze would feel like, cadet? Well, it's nothing like the wind we have here on Earth. Instead, it's a stream of electrically charged (and highly dangerous!) particles flowing at speeds of up to 500 miles per second (800 km/s). Luckily the Earth has a magnetic field (see page 22) that blocks these particles—because this isn't the kind of breeze you'd want to feel on your face!

GO, SOHO!

Many of our most dazzling images of the Sun come from an out-of-this-world observatory called SOHO (short for Solar and Heliospheric Observatory). The SOHO spacecraft, launched in 1995, is about a million miles away from Earth. It enjoys an uninterrupted view of the Sun and provides daily images for scientists studying the Sun's features and behavior.

SOHO scientists (like the one you'll meet on page 13) continue to discover new things about the Sun (like tornadoes on its surface!) and have an up-close view of its other features, which include:

The SOHO spacecraft

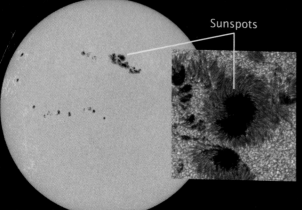

Sunspots

This is the Sun in visible light.

■ **Sunspots:** These dark spots are sometimes found on the surface of the Sun. They look darker because they're cooler areas.

■ **Solar flares:** These are violent explosions in which hot gases shoot out of the Sun's surface, like a cork from a bottle. These flares, which often occur near sunspots, release enormous amounts of high-energy particles that can be very dangerous for astronauts and satellites in space.

Solar flare

Solar prominence

■ **Solar prominences:** These are streams of solar gas held above the Sun's surface by the Sun's magnetic field. They can loop and dance around the Sun, creating arches. They can last for weeks, just hanging there in space, slowly raining back to the Sun.

So what's the big deal about these sunspots and solar prominences anyway? Well, apart from being really *hot* stuff, they're really *huge*, too! How big are we talking about? Size 'em up for yourself and see!

Launch Objective

> See how sunspots and solar prominences compare to Earth!

Your equipment

▶ **Plain piece of paper**
▶ **Pencil**

Part 1: Spot the Sunspots!

1 Here's an image of the Sun with the Earth right beside it.

2 Can't see the Earth? That's because the Sun is soooo much bigger! The Earth is only *this* big (•) compared to a Sun of this size. You could fit 109 Earths across the Sun!

3 Below is an Earth ruler you can use to measure the features of the Sun compared to the Earth. Hold the edge of a piece of paper up to the ruler and mark the notches on your paper.

4 Now use your new ruler to measure the sunspots on the Sun. How many Earths would fit across each one? You can check your answers on page 48!

51zE UP!

Part 2: The Golden Arch

1 Here's another image of the Sun. This image looks different from the first Sun image because it was taken with an *ultraviolet* camera. Ultraviolet (UV) light is invisible to the human eye, but special instruments can detect it. The brighter areas are active regions where a lot of UV light is being emitted. The darker areas are less active.

2 Check out the huge solar prominence that's jutting out of the Sun. How many Earths tall is it? Use your Earth ruler to find out. Put the end of the ruler on the edge of the Sun and measure to the farthest point of the prominence. You can check your answer on page 48.

More from Mission Control

What's a solar storm? A solar storm happens when the Sun spits out a giant bubble of *really* hot gas, called a "coronal mass ejection" (CME), that sends highly charged particles speeding toward the Earth. It's kind of like a big solar burp! If you want to see one of these happen, then hop over to the Space U web site (www.scholastic.com/space), where you can watch movies of the Sun in action! You'll also find a link to today's space weather forecast (which includes the current speeds of solar winds and the latest images of the Sun!).

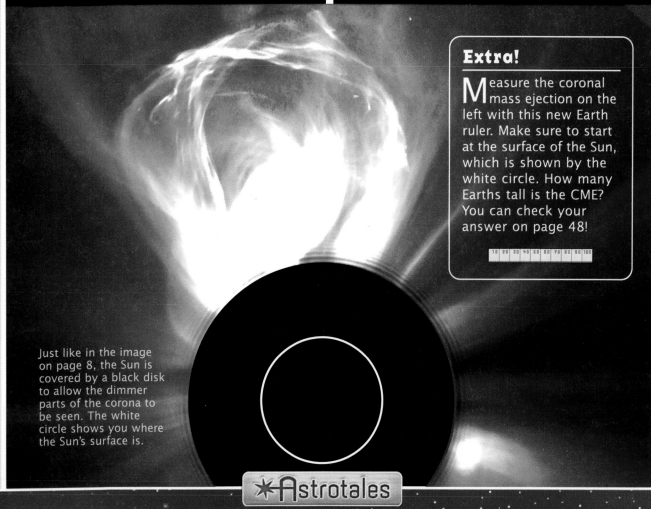

Just like in the image on page 8, the Sun is covered by a black disk to allow the dimmer parts of the corona to be seen. The white circle shows you where the Sun's surface is.

Extra!

Measure the coronal mass ejection on the left with this new Earth ruler. Make sure to start at the surface of the Sun, which is shown by the white circle. How many Earths tall is the CME? You can check your answer on page 48!

`10 20 30 40 50 60 70 80 90 100`

★ Astrotales

Sun Storm!

When a solar storm takes place, you don't need to run for cover! Solar storms usually aren't felt at all here on Earth, thanks to our protective magnetic field (which you can read about on page 22).

But sometimes big solar storms can cause problems on Earth. In March 1989, a powerful flare and a coronal mass ejection sent a huge amount of UV light and highly-charged particles speeding toward the Earth. What happened? When the particles hit the Earth's magnetic field, they interrupted radio broadcasts and satellite signals. Even worse, the changes in the Earth's magnetic field affected the electrical currents in power and telephone lines on the ground, and this knocked out the power in two cities in Canada for up to nine hours!

SOLAR PHYSICIST
Paal Brekke

Meet Dr. Paal Brekke, a solar physicist (a Sun scientist) who's been working on the SOHO mission since 1993. Dr. Brekke helped to design the SOHO spacecraft and analyze its very first solar images.

Question: Why did you decide to study the Sun?

Answer: The Sun is the only star we can observe in detail. It's fascinating to study a star up close!

Q: Why is SOHO so important?

A: SOHO is the biggest and most complex solar observatory satellite ever built. Getting out in space has given us new eyes to see things we never saw before.

Q: What are the biggest SOHO discoveries of all time?

A: We've discovered gigantic jet streams and currents on the Sun. With SOHO, we have also been able to determine where solar wind comes from for the first time (from magnetic fields near the Sun's poles).

Q: How will these discoveries help us on Earth?

A: We believe the Sun is more active now than it was 150 years ago, which means that the Sun is also responsible for global warming. To predict the Earth's climate in the future, we need to know what the Sun will be doing in 50 to 100 years.

Q: Where did SOHO disappear to for four months in 1998?

A: We lost contact with it and didn't know if it was still in its orbit. Luckily, it was still there, but turned around so its solar panels were facing away from the Sun. Without power, it shut down.

Q: How did you fix SOHO without going into space?

A: We managed to get in contact with it, and then we got the solar panels working, thawed the frozen fuel, and pointed SOHO toward the Sun again. I think this will go down in history as one of the most remarkable space rescue operations of all time.

Q: How long will the SOHO mission continue?

A: The SOHO mission will continue until 2007. Once we turn off SOHO, the spacecraft will not come back to Earth. It'll probably drift out of its orbit and into space.

Q: What are the biggest challenges of the SOHO project?

A: The biggest challenge is to keep the spacecraft running for another several years. It is in a very tough environment and so far away from Earth (four times farther than the Moon!) that we can't go up there and repair it if it breaks. Another challenge is to get more young scientists, students, and kids involved. We get so much information from SOHO that we can't use it all ourselves!

All of these images of the Sun were taken by SOHO's extreme ultraviolet telescope. By using different filters, scientists can see the various layers of the Sun's atmosphere. Each color represents a different layer. The orange image is the deepest view, then blue is higher up, and green is even higher.

BEAD DAZZLED

There's a lot more to sunlight than meets the eye. The light you can see is only *part* of the picture—the Sun also sends out other kinds of light that humans *can't* see, like ultraviolet (UV) light (which causes sunburns!). Want to see what you're missing? Then give your ultra-cool UV detector beads a moment in the Sun and see what happens!

Launch Objective

▷ **Use your UV beads to detect invisible UV light.**

Your equipment

▶ **A sunny day**
▶ **UV beads** SPACE CASE
▶ **Bowl**
▶ **Water**
▶ **Window**
▶ **Sun block lotion**
▶ **Sunglasses**

Mission Procedure

1 Start your mission indoors, away from a window. Check out your UV beads. They're kind of pale and boring now, right? Not for long!

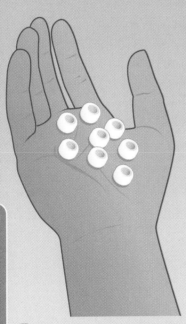

2 Put your UV beads under a lamp and see if anything happens. Do they change color? Just wait....

3 Now head outside where the Sun is shining and hold your beads in the sunlight. Are their true colors shining through? Congratulations, cadet! You've just detected the presence of UV light!

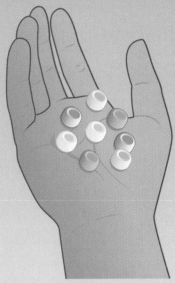

4 Now you can use your beads to test what kinds of materials block UV light. Since UV light can cause sunburns and eye damage, this is good information to have!

■ **Water?** Put some beads in a wide, shallow bowl of water and put the bowl outside in the Sun to see if the beads change.

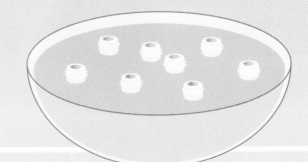

- **Glass?** Hold your beads next to a window where the Sun shines in and see what happens. What about a car window?

- **Sun block lotion?** Smear some lotion on the beads and see if they change color in the Sun. Make sure you smooth the lotion in so the beads aren't white (in which case you wouldn't see the color)!

- **Sunglasses?** Lay some beads on the ground and shade them with your sunglasses. How well do your sunglasses block UV light?

More from Mission Control

Try taking your UV beads outside on a cloudy day. Do they change color? What does this tell you about the protection that cloud cover offers from UV light?

Science, Please!

How do your UV beads work? They're filled with a special chemical that only reveals its color when exposed to UV light. The beads aren't affected by regular visible light, which is why they stay white when they're indoors, away from UV light.

What did you notice from your experimenting with the UV beads? Here's what our Sun experts at Space U discovered. See if your results match up!

- **Direct sunlight:** The UV beads instantly turn bright colors.

- **Sunny window:** The UV beads change color a little slower and are slightly less bright. This means that regular glass provides a *little* protection from the Sun's UV light, but not much.

- **Water:** The UV beads change color just as quickly as without the water, which means that being in a shallow pool or swimming in the ocean won't protect you from UV rays.

- **Sunglasses:** Most sunglasses have a special coating that blocks UV rays, which can harm your eyes. Under sunglasses with good UV protection, the UV beads should change color only slightly, to a pastel shade. You can use your UV beads to test different pairs of sunglasses to see which ones protect your eyes best!

- **Car windows:** Like sunglasses, most car windows are UV treated. Your beads should not have changed color much.

- **Sun block lotion:** The UV beads change color only slightly, which means that your lotion (we used SPF 45) is working to block the Sun's rays.

- **Cloudy day:** The UV beads still change color, although not nearly as much or as quickly as they do on a sunny day. That means that you should still wear your sunscreen even when it's cloudy outside!

SHADOW TIME

Mission Procedure

> As the Earth spins on its axis, the position of the Sun changes. This means your shadow moves, grows, and shrinks. Long ago, people actually *used* these shadow changes to tell time! Try this mission to see what that's all about!

Launch Objective

> Make a working Sun clock and tell time with shadows!

Your equipment

- Action figure or other small object
- Flashlight
- Sun Clock Log pages, printed from the Space U web site
- Scissors
- Piece of cardboard a little bigger than the Sun clock
- Glue
- 7 inches (18 cm) of string
- Tape
- Watch

Part 1: Shady Character

1 Dim the lights in the room, place your action figure on a table, and shine the flashlight down on it.

2 Move the flashlight back and forth over the action figure's head, just like the Sun moves in the sky. What happens to the figure's shadow as the "Sun" arcs across the "sky"? Where do you have to put the flashlight to make the *longest* shadow? And what happens when the "Sun" is directly over the figure's head?

3 Now that you're better acquainted with the world of shadows, move on to the next part of this mission to see how changes in shadows can be used to tell time!

Part 2: Clock Time!

1 Visit the Space U web site (www.scholastic.com/space) and print out the Sun Clock Log pages.

2 Pick the Sun clock that works for your location.

3 Cut out your Sun clock and glue it to a piece of cardboard (or any heavy paper).

4 Cut the little notches marked at the top and bottom of the clock.

5 Fold the clock along the dotted line so the Sun side sticks straight up.

6 Stick one end of the string into the bottom notch and tape the end of the string to the underside of the clock.

7 Stretch the string to the top of the clock and slide it through the notch.

8 Tape the end of the string to the back of the clock. Your correctly set up Sun clock should look like this:

9 Go outside at any hour, *exactly* on the hour, and find a flat area that's free from shadows cast by buildings or trees.

10 Place your Sun clock on the ground, and rotate it until the shadow of the string falls on the correct hour. Which direction is your clock facing? North, south, east, or west? Ask an IGA (Intergalactic Adult) if you're not sure.

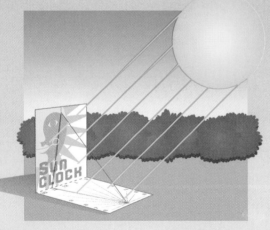

11 Tape your Sun clock down so it won't move, and every hour, go outside and check to see where the shadow is. Does it match up with the time shown on your watch? If not, check your Sun Clock Log pages for some tips that'll help you get better results.

Science, Please!

Before we had mechanical clocks (which were invented about a thousand years ago), people had to use other things to tell time, and what can you count on to move regularly every day? The SUN! So people built huge Sun clocks called *sundials*. Now you have your very own, small enough to fit in your pocket!

When you use your Sun clock again, make sure to place it on the ground facing in the same direction it faced in this mission. It should face *south* if you're in the Northern Hemisphere (in the United States, Canada, or Europe, for example), or *north* if you're in the Southern Hemisphere (in Australia or New Zealand). That's because the Sun is *south* of you in the Northern Hemisphere and *north* of you in the Southern Hemisphere (unless you're really close to the Equator), as you can see in the picture below.

This sundial says it's about 6:00 a.m. The time is indicated by the pointy part of the shadow.

Part 2: Roll with the Third Rock!

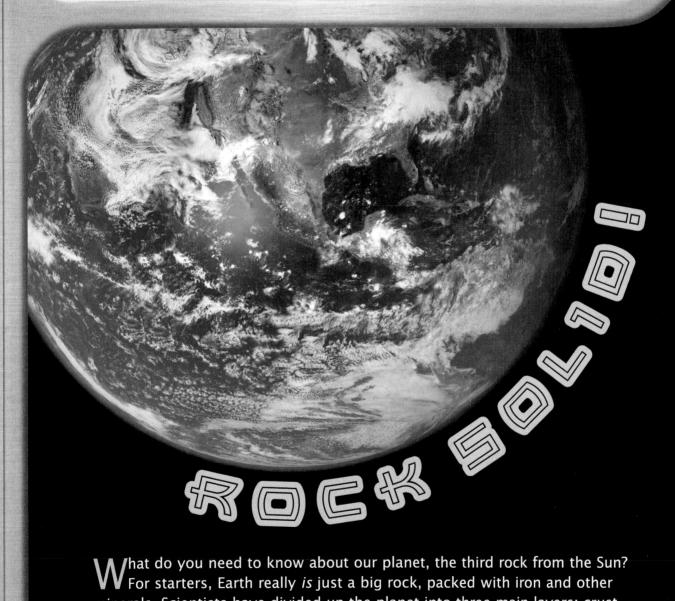

ROCK SOLID!

What do you need to know about our planet, the third rock from the Sun? For starters, Earth really *is* just a big rock, packed with iron and other minerals. Scientists have divided up the planet into three main layers: crust, mantle, and core. If you imagine the Earth as a big juicy apple, the crust is the skin, the mantle is the fleshy part you eat, and the core is—you guessed it—the core! The crust includes all the Earth's surface features, including its highest

mountains and deepest oceans. Anywhere from 4 to 44 miles (7 to 70 km) below the surface (depending on where you dig) is the mantle— a 1,800-mile (2,900-km) thick layer of extremely hot rock that's melted and gooey in some areas. But the core of the Earth is where things *really* heat up—it's even hotter than the surface of the Sun! This core has an outer part that's liquid and an inner part that's squeezed so tight that it's a solid ball of metal.

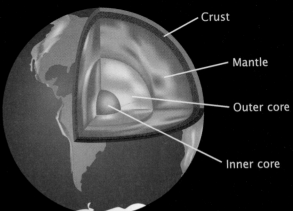

Crust

Mantle

Outer core

Inner core

CAN YOU DIG IT?

How do we know what's inside the Earth? Well, it's not because we dug into the center of it—or anywhere close to it! In fact, the deepest that humans have *ever* drilled into the Earth is a measly 9 miles (15 km). And the entire journey to the center of the Earth is about 3,950 miles (6,357 km)! Scientists have learned almost all we know about the Earth's core from earthquake vibrations (known as "seismic waves") around the world. When an earthquake happens on one side of the planet, certain kinds of waves can pass through liquid and make it through the Earth to be measured on the other side. By studying these special waves, scientists figured out which parts of the Earth are liquid and which parts are solid.

GROOVY GASES

What makes the Earth the perfect place for you and your fellow Earthlings to live is its atmosphere—layers of air that trap some of the Sun's rays and block out the rest, keeping you and a few billion other people warm (but not fried!). These layers of air work just like your favorite blanket on a cold night.

The atmosphere stays around us because of the Earth's gravity—it traps a bunch of gases and holds them in place. These gases include the air that we breathe and a form of oxygen called ozone—which is famous for protecting us from the ultra-strong ultraviolet (UV) rays of the Sun. Our atmosphere is thickest with gases on the bottom and thinner as you head out toward space.

The layers of Earth's atmosphere

53 miles (85 km)   **Mesosphere**

30 miles (50 km)   **Stratosphere**

Ozone layer

9 miles (15 km)   **Troposphere**

Surface

WHY IS THE

What would happen if the Earth had no atmosphere, like the Moon? The sky would always look as black as the blackest night. Really! It's because we have an atmosphere that the sky is blue (on sunny days at least!). But have you ever wondered *why* the sky is blue and not green or some other color? Try this mission and find out!

Launch Objective

> Make your very own mini-atmosphere to see why the sky is blue.

Your equipment

- Large, clear glass or jar
- Water
- Flashlight
- Piece of white paper
- Small amount of milk
- Dropper or small spoon

Mission Procedure

1 Go into a room that you can darken.

2 Pour water into your glass until it's almost full.

3 Turn out the lights and shine your flashlight through the glass, holding the white paper on the other side. You'll see a "Sun" from your flashlight beam shining on the paper.

4 Now add a single drop of milk to the glass and stir it in. Shine the flashlight through the glass again and see what happens. What color is the water with the milk in it? And what color is the flashlight Sun on the paper?

5 Repeat step 4, adding more and more drops of milk to the glass, and observe what happens to your "Sun" shining on the paper.

SKY BLUE?

So, what makes the sky blue? Well, the Sun produces white light, which is really made up of all the colors of the rainbow: red, orange, yellow, green, blue, and purple. Each of these colors has a different *wavelength* (remember wavelengths from your first month at Space U?).

When rays of sunlight head toward us, they have to pass through the atmosphere before we see them. Because of the particular wavelength of blue light, it gets scattered all around the sky by the gases in the atmosphere. That's why we see the sky as blue! The Sun appears to be yellow (which is white light minus blue).

In your experiment, the particles of milk acted like the gases in the atmosphere, scattering the blue light. The milky water was probably only *faintly* blue, but you should have been able to see a *real* difference in the "Sun" projected on your white paper. It should have been white when the flashlight was shined through clear water, but yellow or orange when the flashlight was shined through the milky water. That's because the milk particles were scattering the blue light, so the light that came through was missing its blue!

Have you ever wondered why the Sun looks *more* orange during sunsets? That's because the light has to pass through more atmosphere to reach us when the Sun is low in the sky. As you added more milk to the water, you should have seen the Sun get more orange on your paper.

When other stuff gets into the atmosphere (like big pieces of dust from a volcano or smog from a city), even *more* blue light gets removed, leaving more of the red light around. That means you see beautiful orange or even pinkish-red sunsets.

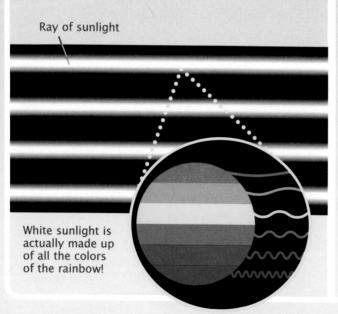

Ray of sunlight

White sunlight is actually made up of all the colors of the rainbow!

THE ULTIMATE SUN BLOCK

Our atmosphere protects us from the Sun's light rays, but it's not enough to shield us from the more serious stuff the Sun throws at us. That's when the *magnetosphere* comes to the rescue! As you can probably tell from the name, the magnetosphere is the Earth's protective magnetic field. Try this mission to see how it works!

Launch Objective

> Use your globe to model the Earth's magnetosphere in action.

Your equipment

▶ **Earth globe (inflated)** SPACE Case
▶ **Thin paper (like newspaper)**
▶ **Scissors**
▶ **Tape**
▶ **Hair dryer**

Personnel

▶ **A friend to hold the Sun (the hair dryer!)**

Mission Procedure

1 Cut the paper into about ten long, thin strips. They should be about ¾ inch (2 cm) wide, and half of the strips should be 16 inches (41 cm) long, the other half 2 feet (61 cm).

2 Tape one end of each paper strip to the Earth's North Pole and the other end to the South Pole. Put all the long strips on one side of the globe and all the short strips on the other.

3 Hold the globe away from your body with the longer strips on the side near you. Get your friend to stand about 3 feet (1 m) away from you and blow the hair dryer toward your globe. What happens to your Earth's "magnetic field"?

Note: The hot air from your hair dryer *acts* like solar wind in this mission, but *real* solar wind is made of high-energy particles (like electrons), *not* hot air.

4 Experiment with the speed of the hair dryer and the distance that it is from "Earth" to see what shape the magnetic field takes. Since the power of hair dryers can vary, it's important to keep experimenting.

Science, Please!

Because the Earth's core is made of hot metal, it makes our planet act like a magnet. This magnet creates a protective region around the Earth, called a "field," that deflects the Sun's high-energy particles away from us. The force of the Sun's wind pushes on the field, causing it to take on the shape shown below. Did your hair dryer cause your strips to take on a similar shape? Did they flatten on the side nearest the hair dryer, and bow out on the side farthest away from the hair dryer?

As you can see in the image to the left, the force of the solar wind actually *stretches* the Earth's magnetic field on the side opposite the Sun. In your model, you had to use longer strips on the side opposite the hair dryer to give your magnetic field that stretched-out look.

Sun's corona

Solar wind

Earth's magnetic field

✱Astrotales

A Magnetic Personality

Within the Earth's magnetic field are areas known as the Van Allen radiation belts, named after James Van Allen, the space scientist who discovered them. In 1958, Van Allen had the brilliant idea of sending a Geiger counter, a device that detects energy traveling through space, on board the *Explorer 1* satellite. As it orbited Earth, this device discovered the inner radiation belt—an area where huge amounts of electrically charged particles from the Sun are trapped by the Earth's magnetic field.

Van Allen radiation belts

Explorer 1, the first satellite ever launched by the United States, carried a device that measured radiation around the Earth.

Auroras!

So, where do the Sun's high-energy particles go when they hit the Earth's magnetic field? They follow the magnetic field lines and head to the North and South Poles, where they go into the Earth. This causes a beautiful show of lights in the sky as the charged particles hit the gases of our atmosphere, giving the gases energy and causing them to emit light. The sky ends up glowing full of colors, like greens, purples, and reds, which we call auroras. The auroras have special names depending on where they're seen—Northern Lights around the North Pole and Southern Lights around the South Pole.

Auroras can come in lots of different colors, depending on the types of gases involved. Each type of gas glows in its own special color when it becomes energized by the Sun's charged particles.

TILT and WHIRL!

Even though we call it a sphere, the Earth isn't perfectly round like a ball—it's actually a bit *squished*. That's because it spins on its axis, and this whirling motion causes the Earth's middle to bulge out. The axis is an imaginary line that runs through the center of the planet, from one pole to the other. The Earth is actually *tilted* to the side, so its axis is not straight up and down.

As the Earth spins on its axis, you experience day and night. While your part of the Earth is facing the Sun, you have daylight, and while your turf is turned away from the Sun, you have night. As the Earth turns, the Sun appears to move across the sky—but really it only *seems* that way to us as *we* spin.

And just when you thought you were *really* dizzy—there's still more spinning! Not only is the Earth spinning on its axis, it's also orbiting around the Sun. And as we make our yearlong journey around the Sun, we experience seasons. Check out the next page to find out the reason for seasons!

FLASH FACT

Long ago, ancient Egyptians believed that Ra, god of the Sun, would row the Sun across the sky in his boat, making the world change from day to night!

QuickBlast

Check Your Speedometer!

How fast does the Earth spin? It depends on where you are! People near the Earth's big fat middle have to move a much greater distance than people up near the poles. So, even though the Earth rotates all at once, your spinning speed depends on where you are. Just how fast are you going? Check out the map to find the place closest to where you live, and check out your current speed. Whoa! That's pretty fast!

171 miles per hour (275 km/h)

477 mph (768 km/h)

737 mph (1186 km/h)

925 mph (1487 km/h)

1022 mph (1645 km/h)

1022 mph (1645 km/h)

925 mph (1487 km/h)

737 mph (1186 km/h)

477 mph (768 km/h)

171 mph (275 km/h)

NORTH AMERICA

EUROPE

ASIA

AFRICA

SOUTH AMERICA

AUSTRALIA

'TIS THE REASON

True or false:
In the summer, it gets hot because the Sun is closer to us, and in the winter it's colder because the Sun moves farther away. FALSE! Even though that sounds like a pretty reasonable explanation at first, it's not the right one. Read on to find out the real reason we have seasons!

Launch Objective

> **Figure out how sunlight gives us seasons!**

Your equipment

▶ **Flashlight**
▶ **Ruler**
▶ **Tape**
▶ **Sheet of paper**
▶ **Colored pencils or crayons**

Personnel

▶ **A friend with steady hands**

Mission Procedure

1 Tape your flashlight to the top of the ruler.

2 Ask your friend to hold the ruler so the flashlight is pointing straight down onto the paper.

3 Turn on your flashlight and look where the light hits the paper. Outline the circle of light with a colored pencil, and label it STRAIGHT DOWN.

4 Now ask your friend to tilt the ruler a little, without moving where it touches the paper. Outline the light beam on the paper in a different color and label it ANGLE 1.

5 Repeat step 4 while tilting the ruler more and more, labeling each beam of light ANGLE 2, ANGLE 3, and ANGLE 4.

6 What do you notice about the light that hits the paper as the angle changes?

Science, Please!

Our planet is tilted about 23 degrees on its axis, so as it zooms around the Sun on its yearly orbit, the Sun's light hits the Earth at different angles. And what did you find out about how angles affect light? That's right, cadet—the bigger the angle, the more the light is spread out over the ground, which makes the light dimmer. So, when your part of the planet is leaning *away* from the Sun, the light is more angled and the Sun's warmth is more spread out, which makes you feel colder. Brrrr...WINTER! Can you guess what happens when your turf is tilted *toward* the Sun? (Hint: Think sunscreen!)

The Northern and Southern Hemispheres have opposite seasons, because when one half of the planet is tilted *toward* the Sun, the other half is tilted away. Those people who live near the Equator experience pretty direct sunlight all year long, so they stay warm all the time!

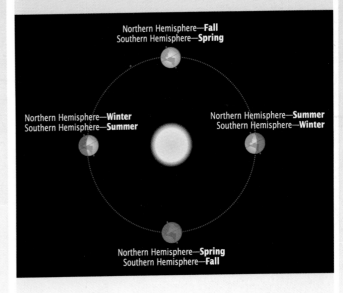

Northern Hemisphere—**Fall**
Southern Hemisphere—**Spring**

Northern Hemisphere—**Winter**
Southern Hemisphere—**Summer**

Northern Hemisphere—**Summer**
Southern Hemisphere—**Winter**

Northern Hemisphere—**Spring**
Southern Hemisphere—**Fall**

Part 3:
Shoot for the Moon

A MOON IN THE MAKING

One day, about 4.5 billion years ago, when our solar system was still being formed, young Earth was happily orbiting the Sun, when—CRASH! A huge planet-sized object, about the size of Mars, smashed into Earth's surface. The crash sent globs of Earth's gooey insides splashing into space, forming a ring of rock around our planet. About half the rock fell back to the Earth. The rest clumped together, and the baby Moon was born!

At first, this young Moon was much closer to the Earth, and it was really big in the sky! But over time, the Moon spiraled away as it lost energy. The Moon *still* moves about an inch away from the Earth every year!

THE BIG CHEESE

Our Moon is pretty hefty as far as moons go. Its *diameter* (its distance across) is about a quarter of the size of the Earth's. You can see this for yourself by comparing your Moon model with your inflated Earth globe. Usually moons are much smaller compared to their planets, which is why we're sometimes called a double planet.

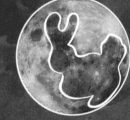

The Moon is made mostly of solid rock, and its powdery surface has a pattern of light and dark areas. The light areas are called the *highlands*. The dark areas are called *seas* (even though there's no water there). The seas were formed when liquid rock flowed over parts of the Moon's surface and hardened.

The Moon is famous for its hundreds of thousands of craters of all shapes and sizes. The craters were formed by *meteorites* (chunks of rock and metal flying through space) that crashed onto the Moon's surface. Since the Moon doesn't have any wind or rain to disturb its surface, its craters stick around for billions of years!

THE MAN IN THE MOON

In the Northern Hemisphere, people see a never-changing pattern of light and dark areas on the face of the Moon that some call the "Man in the Moon." Can you see it? In the Southern Hemisphere, people see the Moon upside down, and they have their own Man in the Moon. Some people in the Southern Hemisphere also see a rabbit.

Northern Hemisphere
Man in the Moon

Southern Hemisphere
Man in the Moon

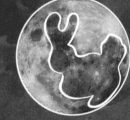

Southern Hemisphere
Rabbit in the Moon

QuickBlast

How Far Is the Moon?

How far away is the Moon from the Earth? Your Earth and Moon models are to scale, which means that they're the same size in relation to each other as the real ones. Imagine how far away the Moon is from Earth like this: Put your

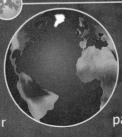

Earth globe on the ground outside in an open area. How many feet away do you think the Moon ball should be to represent how far away the *real* Moon is? Place your Moon at the distance you think it should be, and turn to page 48 to find out if you were right!

TUG OF WAR

We know the Earth's gravity pulls on the Moon. If it didn't, then the Moon would just drift off into space. But did you know that the Moon's gravity also pulls back on the Earth? That's what causes *tides* in our oceans and seas. Tides are changes in water level (which you can see at the beach, when the ocean sometimes seems far away and other times really close).

Tides happen when the Moon pulls on the Earth's water, causing the water to bulge out. As the Earth spins, the bulging areas move across the ocean, causing high and low tides around the world. These tides help more than surfers! Tides make tidal pools (big puddles on the beach), and scientists believe that the first forms of life appeared in these tidal pools. So where would we be if it weren't for the Moon?

And you know what else? The tides *also* create friction that has gradually slowed the Earth's spin over the billions of years since the Moon was formed. So you can thank the Moon for your twenty-four-hour days—without the Moon, you'd have super-short days (the Sun would speed across the sky in about three or four hours!).

QuickBlast

Moonrise

Ever notice how the Moon looks huge while it's on the horizon, and then seems to shrink as it rises? What's up with that? Well, the Moon only *looks* bigger at first because your eyes are playing tricks on you. When you see the Moon on the horizon, it's enormous compared to smaller things on Earth (like mountains, trees, and skyscrapers). As the Moon rises higher in the sky, your brain no longer has anything to compare it to, so it seems smaller.

Check it out for yourself: When there's a full Moon, cover it with your finger early in the evening and see how big it is compared to your finger. Over the next few hours, keep checking to see if it stays the same size as it rises. You'll see that it never really shrinks!

TO THE MOON AND BACK...

Apollo 11 astronaut Buzz Aldrin's bootprint on the Moon's surface

On July 20, 1969, Neil Armstrong declared, "The *Eagle* has landed." The *Eagle* was *Apollo 11*'s lunar module (a special spacecraft designed for Moon landings), and Armstrong and Buzz Aldrin were about to be the very first people ever to set foot on the Moon. The *Apollo 11* mission was the result of the "Space Race," a contest between the United States and the Soviet Union (a country that's now broken up into a bunch of countries, including Russia) to send someone to the Moon. The Soviets were winning, because they sent the first person into space and already had a spacecraft (with no one on board) touch down on the Moon. But that was all about to change as Armstrong steered the *Eagle* down to the Moon's surface and threw open the hatch to take the very first moonwalk in human history.

People all over the world listened to Armstrong's voice and watched him on television as he took his first steps onto the Moon's powdery surface. A few minutes later Aldrin joined him, and the two astronauts had about two hours to explore the Moon.

MOONWALK MADNESS

What would you do if *you* were on the Moon, cadet? Armstrong wasn't sure what to do himself—he said he felt like a five year old in a candy store, with too little time for it all! But he did have enough time to hop around the Moon with Aldrin like a pair of kangaroos, take a bunch of photos, and raise an American flag (which was held up with wire to keep it from drooping on the windless Moon!).

The *Apollo 11* lander

Over the next two hours, the astronauts set up equipment to be left behind on the Moon, including an instrument to detect moonquakes. They also packed up almost 50 pounds (23 kg) of rocks and soil before lifting off from the Moon. When they arrived home, they were greeted as heroes.

The first American flag on the Moon

In the three years after *Apollo 11*, six more Apollo missions went to the Moon. Five of them actually made it to the Moon (*Apollo 13* didn't land because of an explosion on the spacecraft that forced it to return to Earth). With each landing, new discoveries were made about the age, structure, and formation of the Moon. A total of twelve astronauts walked (or drove around in lightweight cars called rovers) on the surface of the Moon. The final manned mission to the Moon was the *Apollo 17* mission in 1972. Some people say it's time to return to the Moon. Maybe *you* could be on board next time!

Astronaut John W. Young jumps as he salutes the American flag on his first *Apollo 16* moonwalk in 1971.

Moon rovers could travel as fast as 11 miles per hour (18 km/h). They were powered by two batteries, and they were able to drive over obstacles up to 1 foot (30 cm) high. Rovers could carry two astronauts (who had to wear special space suits that allowed them to bend at the waist, so they could sit!).

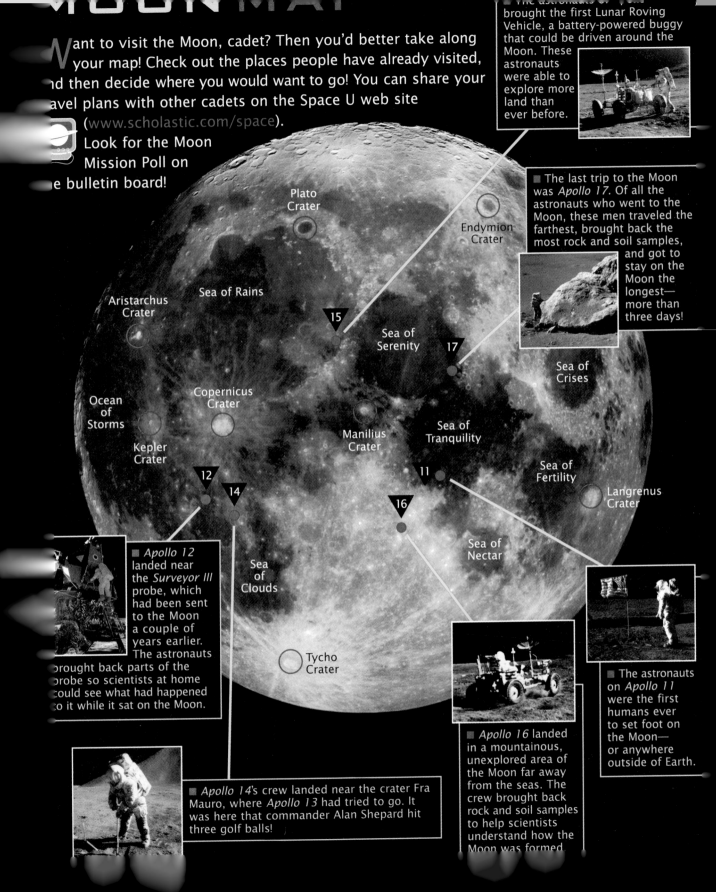

MOON MAP

Want to visit the Moon, cadet? Then you'd better take along your map! Check out the places people have already visited, and then decide where you would want to go! You can share your travel plans with other cadets on the Space U web site (www.scholastic.com/space).

Look for the Moon Mission Poll on the bulletin board!

■ ...brought the first Lunar Roving Vehicle, a battery-powered buggy that could be driven around the Moon. These astronauts were able to explore more land than ever before.

■ The last trip to the Moon was *Apollo 17*. Of all the astronauts who went to the Moon, these men traveled the farthest, brought back the most rock and soil samples, and got to stay on the Moon the longest— more than three days!

■ *Apollo 12* landed near the *Surveyor III* probe, which had been sent to the Moon a couple of years earlier. The astronauts brought back parts of the probe so scientists at home could see what had happened to it while it sat on the Moon.

■ *Apollo 14*'s crew landed near the crater Fra Mauro, where *Apollo 13* had tried to go. It was here that commander Alan Shepard hit three golf balls!

■ *Apollo 16* landed in a mountainous, unexplored area of the Moon far away from the seas. The crew brought back rock and soil samples to help scientists understand how the Moon was formed.

■ The astronauts on *Apollo 11* were the first humans ever to set foot on the Moon— or anywhere outside of Earth.

Plato Crater
Endymion Crater
Sea of Rains
Aristarchus Crater
15
Sea of Serenity
17
Sea of Crises
Ocean of Storms
Copernicus Crater
Manilius Crater
Sea of Tranquility
Sea of Fertility
Kepler Crater
12
14
11
16
Langrenus Crater
Sea of Nectar
Sea of Clouds
Tycho Crater

LEFT BEHIND on the MOON

NASA astronauts left a whole lot more than their footprints and flags behind on the Moon. Apart from the equipment they left, they also had to dump a lot of unneeded stuff to lighten their loads for the trip back to Earth. If you were to visit the Moon today, you'd find more than a hundred items, including:

- Buzz Aldrin and Neil Armstrong's boots and space suits.

- A gold replica of an olive branch, the traditional symbol of peace, left on the Moon by Neil Armstrong to represent a wish for peace for all mankind.

- Three golf balls hit by astronaut Alan Shepard.

- A bunch of scientific equipment.

- An insulating blanket.

- A plaque signed by U.S. President Richard Nixon and the *Apollo 11* astronauts that reads: HERE MEN FROM THE PLANET EARTH FIRST SET FOOT UPON THE MOON JULY 1969 A.D. WE CAME IN PEACE FOR ALL MANKIND.

- A hammer and a bunch of other tools.

- Assorted containers for food, urine, and rock samples.

- At least twelve cameras.

- The bases of all the lunar landing modules.

- Three Moon rovers, worth millions of dollars each!

QuickBlast

Have a Drink on the Moon!

Since the Moon is less massive than the Earth, its gravity is weaker. Because there's less gravity, things feel much lighter on the Moon. If you can pick up a boulder that weighs 50 pounds (23 kg) on Earth (which would make you really strong!), then you could pick up a great big boulder on the Moon that would weigh 250 pounds (113 kg) on Earth (wow!). So, what would a can of soda feel like on the Moon? Try this test to see for yourself!

1 Get two soft-drink cans—one empty, one full.

2 Fill the empty can with nineteen pennies.

3 Lift both cans, one in each hand. The full can is what a can of soda feels like on Earth (of course!). The penny-filled can is how a full can would feel on the Moon!

THE FAR SIDE

You may have heard of the "dark side of the Moon," but really there isn't any such thing! Both sides of the Moon get light from the Sun, but one side, which is correctly called the *far* side, is never seen from Earth. Why? It's *not* because the Moon never turns, because the Moon *does* spin on its axis as it revolves around the Earth. The Moon takes 27 days, 7 hours, and 43 minutes to spin once on its axis—almost the exact time it takes to orbit the Earth. Because of this special spin, we see only one side of the Moon here on Earth. See how this works for yourself with the Quick Blast below.

FIRST GLIMPSE

It wasn't until 1959 that the world got its first peek at the far side of the Moon. That was when the Soviets sent their *Luna 3* spacecraft on a trip around the Moon. *Luna 3* had a camera on board that took photos of the far side and beamed them back to Earth. Scientists discovered that the far side of the Moon looks a lot different from the side that we see all the time—it has more craters and fewer seas (dark spots).

Put Your Best Face Forward

Want to know why we see only one side of the Moon? Then team up with a friend, grab your Earth and Moon, and try this!

1 Have a friend stand facing you, holding your Earth globe.

2 Look at the pictures of both sides of the Moon on this page and on page 32 so you can tell which side of the Moon ball is which. Use a small sticker or piece of tape to mark the Moon's near side, and hold the Moon ball with the near side facing your friend.

3 Try orbiting (walking) around the Earth with the near side of the Moon always pointing toward your friend.

4 Sound easy enough? Well, you also have to spin the Moon around once! Each time you move a quarter of the way around your friend, turn the Moon ball a quarter of the way, too, always keeping its near side pointing toward your friend. That way your Moon is orbiting and spinning at the same rate— just like the real Moon!

MOONDANCE

You've seen the Moon change from looking like a big round melon, to just a slice, and then back to a whole melon again. What makes it seem to grow and shrink? Take the Moon for a spin and find out!

Launch Objective

See what makes the Moon change shape in the sky.

Your equipment

- A lamp with its shade removed, or a desk lamp
- Moon ball

Mission Procedure

1 Turn on the lamp in a darkened room and stand several feet (about 1 m) away from it, holding the Moon ball. The lamp represents the Sun, your head represents the Earth, and the Moon ball is—you guessed it—the Moon!

2 Hold the Moon at arm's length and slowly turn your body around.

3 As your Moon ball orbits your head, stop frequently and observe the way the light reflects off it. Notice the shadows that are formed. Do the shapes you see change like the Moon's shape changes over a month?

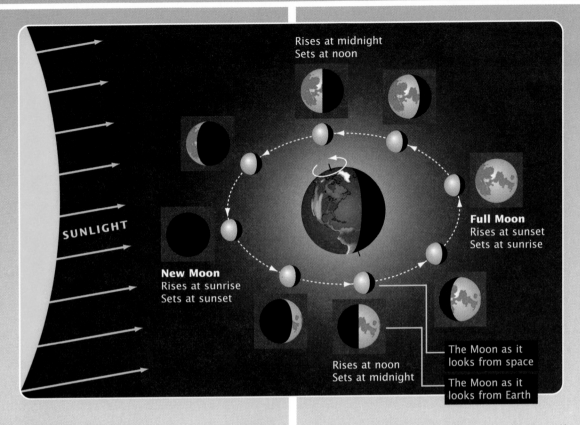

Rises at midnight
Sets at noon

Full Moon
Rises at sunset
Sets at sunrise

SUNLIGHT

New Moon
Rises at sunrise
Sets at sunset

Rises at noon
Sets at midnight

The Moon as it
looks from space

The Moon as it
looks from Earth

Science, Please!

The Moon that brightens the night sky doesn't have any light of its own. The only reason we see it is because the light from the Sun bounces off of it. Just like the Earth, half of the Moon is *always* lit by the Sun, while the other half is dark. The entire Moon is lit up at some point or another, which is why there's no "dark" side, just a *far* side that we don't ever see. As the Moon orbits the Earth over a month, we're able to see different amounts of the near side, which makes it seem like the Moon's shape changes in the sky from full, to half, to crescent, and back to full again.

A full Moon happens each month when the Moon, Earth, and Sun are all lined up in a row (which is known as *syzygy*, pronounced "SIH-zuh-gee"). About twice a year, a lunar eclipse happens when the three bodies are aligned in such a way that the Earth blocks the Sun's light from reaching the Moon. Sometimes the eclipsed

Moon appears dark red because light still reaches it after passing through the edges of Earth's atmosphere, where blue light is scattered (remember this from page 21?). When *all* of the Sun's light is blocked, the Moon seems to vanish. These eclipses don't happen more often because the Moon's path around the Earth is tilted, so it's not usually in perfect alignment with the Earth and Sun.

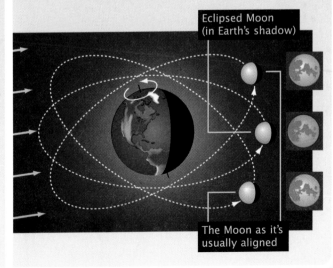

Eclipsed Moon
(in Earth's shadow)

The Moon as it's
usually aligned

CRATER MAKER

The Moon takes a real pounding from meteorites hurtling through space. Want to create your own craters? Then toss a mini-meteorite and see what happens!

Launch Objective

Cook up some craters with a little flour and cocoa.

Your equipment

- Newspaper
- Large shallow bowl or box
- Several cups of white flour (to fill the bottom of the bowl or box)
- Ruler
- Spoon
- $\frac{1}{3}$ cup cocoa powder or powdered chocolate milk mix
- Three balls of various sizes (like a marble, a golf ball, and a super ball)

Mission Procedure

1 Spread the newspaper out on the ground, put your bowl on it, and fill the bowl with about 2 inches (5 cm) of flour. Smooth the flour with a spoon.

2 Sprinkle a thin layer of chocolate powder over the surface of the flour.

3 Now stand above the bowl and drop the smallest ball straight into the bowl. Remove the ball. What do you notice about the crater that was formed? What was thrown out of the crater?

4 Fill in the holes that were made, smooth the top over, and sprinkle on more chocolate powder if needed.

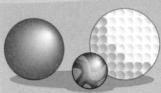

5 Now try dropping each of the larger balls in different areas. Drop them from the same height as you dropped the first ball. What do the craters look like? How do they compare to the first crater?

6 Try dropping the balls from higher above the bowl (which makes the balls land at a higher speed). How does this change the way the craters look?

Moon crater is no ordinary hole. A meteorite headed toward the Moon has a whole lot of energy and speed, and when it crashes into the Moon's surface—poof! The meteorite and the area of the Moon's crust that it hits just vaporize. Then crushed rock gets thrown out, and it falls around the rim of the crater, creating walls and even mountains that can be taller than 5 miles (8 km)—that's taller than Mount Everest! There are also lines of tossed-out material, or rays, that stretch far away from the crater. You should have been able to see white rays of flour on the brown surface around your craters.

You should also have noticed that the size of a crater depended on both the size and speed of the meteorite that formed it. The larger and faster the meteorites, the larger the craters.

Here's a 5-inch (12.5-cm) piece of the huge meteorite that made Meteor Crater (below). It's made of iron and nickel, and its surface is shiny in parts because the meteorite got very hot and melted as it passed through Earth's atmosphere.

★Astrotales

Make Your Mark

The Moon isn't the only object in space that gets clobbered by meteorites. The Earth and other planets have their share of the fun, too! In fact, the Earth would look a lot like the Moon if it weren't for our atmosphere. Most of the meteorites that hurtle toward Earth get burned up in the friction from the atmosphere before they make it to the surface. Also, since we have wind and rain, craters on Earth (most of which were formed billions of years ago) get eroded away over the years.

Even though most of Earth's craters are gone by now, scientists have found evidence of them all over the world by studying the Earth's crust and mantle and finding traces of meteorites. One of the Earth's biggest craters was found in Mexico in the 1990s, and it could help prove that a meteorite impact caused the dinosaurs to die off.

This is Meteor Crater, a 50,000-year-old crater in northeast Arizona. It's about three-quarters of a mile (1 km) wide.

Part 4:
Satellites and Other Space Invaders

WHAT'S A SATELLITE?

Did you know that a satellite is simply any object that orbits something bigger than itself, like a planet or star? Our planet, like all the others in our solar system, is a natural satellite of the Sun. The Moon is the Earth's natural satellite, but it's kept company by about 3,000 man-made satellites hanging outside of our atmosphere in space.

The first man-made satellite was *Sputnik*, launched by the Soviet Union in 1957. As *Sputnik* orbited Earth, it broadcast a faint radio signal, just "beep...beep...beep," and that was pretty much all there was to it (but back then, that was a lot!). Since *Sputnik*, lots of high-tech satellites have been developed to study things like stars, the Earth's atmosphere, our environment, and our weather. Satellites also let us watch television programs from all over the world, and they make it possible for us to find our way around with navigation devices. And of course, they're also used by the military and by intelligence agencies to spy on various parts of the world!

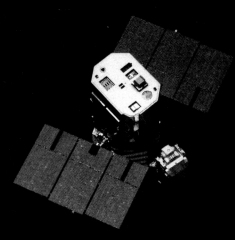

Satellite   Space shuttle cargo bay

Satellites ride into space on top of a rocket or inside the cargo bay of a space shuttle. Here's a picture of a satellite being released from a shuttle's cargo bay.

ANATOMY OF A SATELLITE

Satellites have a lot of high-tech parts, but the most important ones are these:

Cameras or sensors: Satellites take photos or collect data to send back to Earth.

Power collectors: Satellites run on solar power. The huge silver panels collect sunlight.

Communication device: Satellites need to be in touch with command centers on Earth, which is why they have large radio antennae and transmitters.

Body: The outer part of the satellite is built of extra-tough materials to protect it from the heat of the Sun, the cold of space, and any particles flying around that could cause damage.

THIS END IS UP

How do satellites stay in orbit? What keeps them from falling back to Earth or drifting off into space?

Good questions! Here's the scoop: Satellites are launched at just the right speed to keep them in orbit around the Earth. They don't lose this speed because of a force known as *inertia* (pronounced "in-UR-sha"). Inertia is the principle that an object set in motion will stay in motion unless something works to stop it. You can see this principle at work just by looking at how our planet keeps moving around and around the Sun. There's nothing slowing it down (like air or friction), so it keeps going. The same holds true for satellites up in space—once they're out there, they keep going and going and going!

Satellites only work if they're in the exact spot they're supposed to be and facing the right direction. Imagine a satellite that's taking pictures of the Earth—how does it know which way to point in the weightlessness of space? It can't tell up from down! Well, that's where satellites get a little help from a whirling wonder called a gyroscope. What does a gyroscope do? Try the next mission to find out!

GO FOR A SP1N

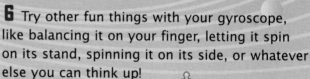

Kind of like a top, but much cooler, a gyroscope really whirls! It also has a great sense of direction, which is why satellites use gyroscopes to keep them pointing the right way in space. Ready to take yours for a spin?

Launch Objective

Set your gyroscope spinning and see what it can do!

Your equipment

▶ Gyroscope
▶ Smooth, flat surface
▶ Hardcover book

SPACE CASE

Mission Procedure

1 Start your gyroscope spinning by inserting the cord. Slide it in so that the side with the teeth is facing the center of the gyroscope.

2 While holding the edges of the gyroscope, quickly pull out the cord.

3 Set the spinning gyroscope down on a smooth surface and watch how it spins. What happens after a while?

4 After the gyroscope stops, set it in motion again, but this time hold it in your hand. Try to turn your hand over and feel the resistance the gyroscope gives you.

5 Place your spinning gyroscope on a hardcover book. Lift the book and tilt it slightly from side to side. How does the gyroscope respond?

6 Try other fun things with your gyroscope, like balancing it on your finger, letting it spin on its stand, spinning it on its side, or whatever else you can think up!

Science, Please!

Have you ever tried to balance on a bike that's standing still? It's almost impossible. But once the bike starts rolling, it becomes easier and easier to stay upright, doesn't it? That's because things that spin are steady, and the faster something spins, the more stable it becomes.

Things floating out in space can roll and tip and spin really easily in all directions. This makes it especially hard to keep equipment in space steady and pointing in one direction—something that all satellites and telescopes have to do. So, to deal with this problem, satellite designers put super-spinning gyroscopes into satellites. If the satellites try to move or tip, the gyroscopes hold them in place. Did you notice how your gyroscope fought back when you tried to turn your hand over? Did you notice how it tried to stay horizontal when you tilted the book? That's the idea!

Satellites equipped with cameras, sensors, and radars give us incredible views of the Earth from space. Would you be able to tell what you were looking at from way up there? See if you can figure it out!

Launch Objective

> Get an out-of-this-world view of Earth's features.

Your equipment

▶ **Your eyeballs**

EYE ON EARTH

Mission Procedure

Look at these images of Earth from space. Can you match each image to one of the following descriptions? You can check your answers on page 48!

1 Volcano
2 Farm fields
3 Brush fires
4 Whirlpool in the ocean
5 Grand Canyon
6 Sahara desert
7 Mount Everest
8 Cyclone (a huge storm)
9 Antarctica
10 Ocean sands
11 Irrigation in the desert
12 New York City

B

C

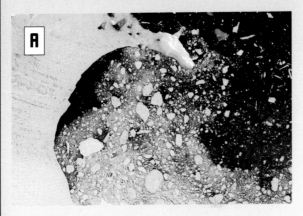

A

D

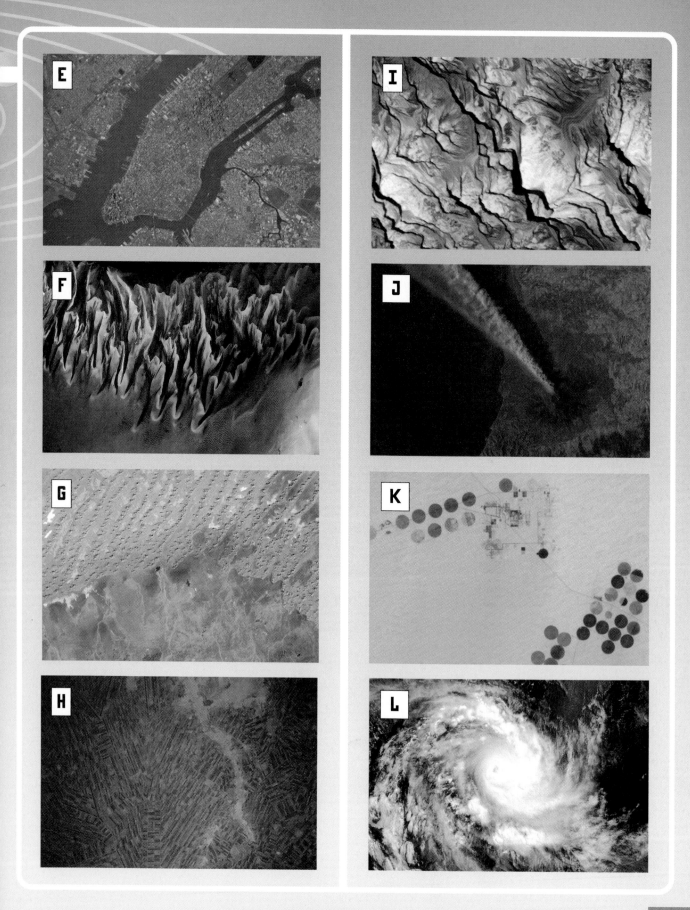

SPACE JUNK!

Ever gazed at the night sky and caught a glimpse of a "shooting star"? Maybe you felt really lucky and made a wish on it. But did you know that a shooting star isn't really a star? Most of the time, it's a chunk of metal or rock flying through the Earth's atmosphere and burning up. But get this: A "shooting star" might also be a piece of *junk*! It's true!

Experts estimate that there's about 4 million pounds (1.8 million kg) of stuff that people left behind, better known as "space junk," orbiting the Earth. This includes old satellites, old rocket parts, and even tiny screws, bolts, and paint chips. Sometimes this junk falls back into Earth's atmosphere and burns up. If it's big enough, a piece of junk might actually make it down to Earth. But don't worry about it falling on your head—most of the junk falls into the ocean, which covers two-thirds of our planet.

WATCH OUT FOR SPEEDING TRASH!

Space junk moves fast—about 17,000 miles per hour (27,360 km/h)! That means that even a really tiny piece of junk, like a fleck of paint from an old rocket, can act like a bullet in space. Want to see how a little speed can give something as small as a quarter some extra *punch*? Then try out the next mission!

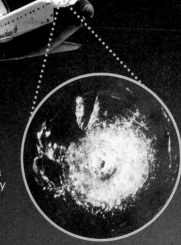

When a tiny paint fleck collided with a space shuttle window, it made a dent about 2 mm wide! That's why shuttle windows have to be carefully checked after each flight, and the windows are often replaced.

DANGER: FLYING TRASH AHEAD!

Flying space junk can be a real threat to spacecraft and astronauts, which is why space suits and other space equipment must be made out of extremely tough materials. Check out how even the smallest objects can cause major damage if they're moving fast enough!

Launch Objective

> See how a small flying object can make a big impact!

Your equipment

- **Large plastic cup**
- **Tissue**
- **Rubber band**
- **Quarter**
- **Ruler**

Mission Procedure

1 Lay a tissue over the mouth of your cup.

2 Secure the tissue with the rubber band, making sure the tissue is stretched tight.

3 Prop the ruler against a wall and place your cup near it.

4 From a height of 2 inches (5 cm) above the cup, drop the quarter onto the tissue. What happens?

5 Now try making the quarter hit the tissue at a higher speed by releasing it from 4 inches (10 cm) above the cup. What happens now?

6 Keep increasing the speed of the quarter by dropping it from 6 inches (15 cm), and then 8 inches (20 cm), and then higher and higher. At what height does the tissue break?

Science, Please!

Ever have a friend accidentally bump into you? What happens if your friend is running instead of walking? It hurts more, doesn't it? Speed can make anything become dangerous. In this mission, you saw how your quarter was able to punch through the tissue when it was traveling fast. In space, orbiting junk travels at super-high speeds, so even a little piece of it, like a paint chip, can pack a big punch.

So, how do we protect our spacecraft and astronauts from flying junk? Well, first of all, even though there's a lot of junk out there, the space around Earth is *still* really empty (because it's so huge!), so the chances of hitting a piece of junk are slim. But still, we track all the big pieces so we can avoid them on space missions, and we make sure spacecraft and space-walking astronauts are protected by extra-tough materials. An astronaut's space suit is actually made of bullet-proof fabric!

Part 5:
Fast-Forward to the Future!

Let's fast-forward a few billion years into the future and see how the Earth's neighborhood might look....

FORECAST: BIG RED SUNNY DAYS!

Lucky for us Earthlings, we can count on the Sun doing its thing for many years to come. The average life span of a star like our Sun is about 11 billion years. Since the Sun's been shining for only 4.5 billion years so far, it has about 5 or 6 billion years left!

What'll happen after 5 or 6 billion years? Well, as the Sun finally runs low on energy, its core will shrink and the outer layers will expand and cool. At this point the Sun will become what's known as a *red giant* star. The red giant will spread beyond the Earth's orbit, vaporizing anything in its path. After that, it will slowly shrink until it becomes a *white dwarf* (a tiny star) about the size of the Earth. The entire process will take a few billion years.

Good Night, Moon!

As you've heard by now, the Moon is slowly spiraling away from the Earth. After billions of years, the Moon will be quite a bit farther from Earth than it is now. What other weird things will happen? Check out the comic strip below!

The moon spirals away...

See ya!

Hey, where ya goin'?

As the Moon backs off, the Earth will spin slower. That means that one day on Earth will be as long as about fifty-five of our current days! Plus, the Earth will start wobbling as it slows down!

Is this day dragging on or what?

Eventually, the Moon will always sit over the same spot on the Earth, so only half of the people on Earth will ever see the Moon! But then things get really exciting....

Hey, where's the Moon?

The motion of the tides will give the Moon a kick in the opposite direction, and it will start spiraling back toward Earth! But don't worry, it won't crash into Earth...

INCOMING!

...when it gets too close to Earth, it'll get ripped apart by the Earth's gravity...

eep...

...and all those pieces of the Moon will make a ring around our planet. So, Earth will have something in common with Saturn! But this might never have a chance to happen—the Sun might run out gas before we ever get our lunar ring.

Smashing new ring, Earth!

Why, thank you!

We are Family!

Wow, cadet! You've been on one wild ride around Earth's neighborhood! You've traveled to the far side of the Moon, dug deep into the Earth, and checked out the surface of the Sun! You've also learned how Earth's neighborhood is one big whirling family (with its fair share of family drama!).

The next time you gaze up at the Moon or feel the warmth of the Sun on your face, remember that we're all working and moving together in our solar system. And remember that the Earth is more than just a pretty blue planet—it's totally fortified to keep you safe from all the harshness of space. So be glad! And don't forget to do your part to keep your planet clean and healthy for years to come. It's the only home we've got—at least for now!

So, we'll see you after another set of Moon phases for your next round of Space U training!

THE ANSWER STATION

■ Pages 10–12: **Sunny Size Up!**

Part 1

This group of sunspots is about 19 Earths long. All others are 1 or 2 Earths long.

Part 2

This prominence is about 28 Earths long.

More from Mission Control

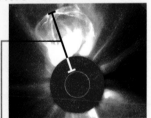

The coronal mass ejection is about 300 Earths long.

■ Page 28: **How Far Is the Moon?**

The Moon should be about 20 feet (6 m) away from the Earth.

■ Page 42: **Eye on Earth**
1) J   2) H   3) C   4) D   5) B   6) G   7) I   8) L   9) A   10) F   11) K   12) E